Insider Secrets From A Hollywood Pro

111 Star Power Tips

For

Videos, Audios,
On-Camera Interviews,
TV, Radio & Presentations

By Barbara Niven

Hollywood's Top Media Trainer
Business Presentation Coach
Best-Selling Author
Actress & Speaker

UnleashYourStarPower.com

First Printing October 2011
Printed in the U.S.A.

 ISBN-13: 978-1460912331

Visit Unleash Your Star Power and Barbara Niven on the World Wide Web
http://www.unleashyourstarpower.com
http://www.barbaraniven.com

Edited by: Kim Ross
Creative Direction and Design by Shadoeworks®
Published by Shadoeworks®
http://www.shadoeworks.com

Barbara Niven's
UNLEASH YOUR STAR POWER!™
Home Study Course
For
Videos, Audios, On-Camera Interviews, TV, Radio & Presentations

- *Handle Nerves & Turn Them in to Fuel*
- *Learn Exactly What to Say & How to Say It*
- *Excel in TV & Radio Interviews*
- *Discover How to Hook Your Audience Instantly*
- *Create Your Message & Talking Points*
- *Speak in Sound Bites*
- *Develop Your Voice into a Powerful Instrument*
- *Get Preparation Secrets That Guarantee Success*
- *Build Skills to Present & Perform Like a Pro*
- *Be Thrilled with Your Confidence and New Professional Image!*

Need great videos? Come to our L.A. studio.
Barbara will personally coach & direct you on-camera!
Custom video production services available

UnleashYourStarPower.com   1-855-STAR POWER

About Barbara Niven

Barbara Niven is one of Hollywood's busiest actresses, and has more than 2500 TV, film and commercial roles to her credit. You've seen her starring on Lifetime, Hallmark, NCIS, Cold Case and One Life to Live. Barbara was elected to and served on the National Board of Directors for the Screen Actors Guild. She also is in demand as a Media Trainer, Performance Coach, Speaker, and Best-Selling Author.

Barbara created and developed *Unleash Your Star Power!*™ to share her professional skills and unique talents with others. From her studio in Los Angeles, she offers custom video production services, one-on-one coaching and workshops, and is available for speaking engagements. Her clients include business owners, CEOs, entrepreneurs, speakers, authors, and anyone who wants to makeover their professional image.

www.UnleashYourStarPower.com
www.BarbaraNiven.com
1-855-STARPOWER

This book is dedicated to my sister, Kim.
I am so grateful you are in my life.

www.UnleashYourStarPower.com

Thank You

Thank you to the people in my life who have helped me shine. To my parents, George and Edie, who taught this chubby little blonde girl to believe everything is possible. To my sister, Kim, for proving that nothing is more important than family. She went through every word in this book and made it, and me, better. To my beautiful daughter, Jess, who teaches me every day about love and integrity, and to her husband Joerg, my favorite musician. To Kathy for believing in me all these years, and for her brilliant design skills that launch our dreams. To Jack for helping me hone my message, and who has been there from the beginning. To James for mentoring me to take it to the next level. To Kristin for her light and inspiration. To Susan, Gail and Joyce for endless love, support and guidance. And to Phyllis, who laughs and cries with me through thick and thin, no matter what.

Testimonials

What people are saying about Barbara Niven and *Unleash Your Star Power!*

"My fear of speaking in front of a camera was limiting my potential. Barbara is the best in her field. A true professional, she knows her business start-to-finish in every aspect of production, from performance to finished product. She directs, guides and coaches you to hone your message and performance. She made the process so easy. I highly recommend her to anyone looking to launch their career to new heights and possibilities. Barbara's number one gift is that she can bring out yours!"
Brian C. Traichel, Director of Business Development, Brian Tracy International

"Thanks to Barbara's extraordinary training, I now speak internationally. Her media training has given me the skills to attract press to my business on a regular basis; as my client's media spokesperson, it allows me to make additional revenue. If you're ready to kick-up your performance to the next level, call Barbara Niven."
Denise Turner, Business Consultant & Speaker

"YOU ARE THE MOST AMAZING VIDEO COACH EVER!!! I still can't believe how many videos we were able to shoot in an hour because your 20-minutes of pre-shoot coaching were so masterful. You make the intimidating experience of talking into a camera a fun and powerful one for getting my message out to the world."
Rosemary Bredeson, Entrepreneur

Testimonials (continued)

"Prior to taking the class, I was stuck in terms of how I would best present my message. After three days in the Bootcamp, I am now bursting with ideas and confidence. Barbara is the expert in video skills, marketing, storytelling, and knowing how to ignite your audience and have fun. I highly recommend this class to anyone who needs public speaking and/or videos to promote their business."
Kristin Macdonald, Radio Show Host & Speaker

"Because of your instruction and feedback, I went from hiding behind my boring PowerPoint presentation to being comfortable and authentic with my audience, trusting that the right words and presence will come forth to make it a rich and meaningful experience for them. And I'm having fun, too!"
Melinda Dewey, Small Business Owner

"Barbara is an expert in getting our sound bites, our video and our message out to the world. Even if you're a little nervous in front of the camera, she's the lady to see. She shot my videos and I had a ball! I was so at ease in front of the camera and I've never been that way before. I highly recommend her and I'm thrilled she's part of our Premiere Mentorship Program."
Marsh Engle, Entrepreneur, Founder of Amazing Woman's Day

"Barbara gave me the tools and techniques I needed to prepare properly for the spotlight events that any musician will face at one time or another. Whether it's your very first interview with a local newspaper, telling a compelling story between songs, your acceptance speech at the Grammys or your chat with David Letterman on the tonight show. ;) Don't leave your career up to chance, be prepared."
Joerg Kohring, Musician & Composer, Teacher at Musician's Institute, Los Angeles

Testimonials (continued)

"Barbara, thank you for sharing your experience, your insight and your wisdom. It's hard to believe that only a few short years ago I had major issues with public speaking/cameras...even mirrors. Thanks to you, I went from terrified to confident my first time on camera. The tools you supplied me with, the tricks and hints you taught me, everything we did together came back to me on shoot day - I felt you there with me! You are the best and I am looking forward to continuing working with you."
Tina Fanelli Moraccini, Small Business Owner & TV Show Host

"It was such an amazing experience to work with you the other day, Barbara. I just wanted to let you know that the process really gave me insights on how I show up in the world. Watching myself on the monitor and seeing the difference of expression and vitality in me as I was more myself was actually quite cathartic. It was such a breakthrough that after our session I was able to get back in touch with the Italian in me and bring her out more often. It certainly was a learning lesson and I appreciate you "literally" holding my hand through it."
Micaela Passeri, Clothing Designer & Small Business Owner

"I have taken two of Barbara's workshops. She is full of enthusiasm and energy and shows infinite patience as she takes each of the participants through how to create their video message. Each time she mentions an improvement to one person, it is a lesson for all of us in the audience. This was my second workshop and there was such a dramatic improvement to my performance! Barbara works magic!"
Patsy Bellah, Small Business Owner, Information Marketer

Star Power Tip #1

Video is exploding as a business tool. If you're not using it yet, your competitors are. However, poor quality video is worse than no video at all, because image is everything. You probably are very good at what you do, but if you're not good in front of the camera, it's the first thing people notice. We're a media savvy society and you will be judged against the professionals on TV. Even if you're an expert in your field, poor on-camera skills may question your credibility, tagging you as unprofessional, amateurish or even "shifty." ***Make sure you're sending the right message*** to your potential clients. Learn the basics – it makes all the difference!

Star Power Tip #2

Turn nerves into fuel to drive a better performance! Actors learn to handle anxieties in order to perform or audition, and you can too. Milton Katselas, renowned teacher and founder of the Beverly Hills Playhouse, taught ***nerves and excitement both manifest themselves in the same way... via heart palpitations, hyperventilation, and butterflies in the stomach.*** So consider this. What if, instead of labeling these as fear, you ***perceive them as excitement*** for your upcoming performance? Interesting, huh? It works! Next time nerves hit, shift your attitude and shift your reality. Become a racehorse at the starting gate, raring to go!

Star Power Tip #3

Lighting is everything in videos. Actors know it can make or break you. Quality lighting makes a huge difference in the end product and how people respond to you emotionally. Make sure to face directly into the main light source so you are fully lit from the front. This will ensure your eyes and face are clearly visible, with no harsh shadows. Otherwise you may come across with subliminal, creepy or unprofessional messages. ***Don't settle for an unflattering shot!*** If needed, move a light, face into a window (a great light source!), change the camera angle, pull the blinds to control daylight, get away from direct sunlight, add a fill light or use a reflector. You'll go from Two Buck Chuck to looking like a million bucks in seconds.

Star Power Tip #4

In a TV interview, don't sit there like a prop, staring stiffly at the host. Most people are afraid to interact with the camera, but if you don't, you'll come across like a deer in headlights. Here's the trick. Think of the camera as the third-party viewer and consider it another person in the room. When you are introduced, smile a sincere "happy-to-see-you" welcome into the camera, then naturally split your looks between the host and camera lens. Make it a 3-way conversation and *include the viewer in the fun*. Assume you're always on-camera – they may cut to your *"close-up"* any time. Don't be afraid to speak up and don't make the interviewer do all the work. Bring energy and personality. Get your points across. Use stories. Be an exciting, entertaining guest!

Star Power Tip #5

Here's why you need video. According to the Wharton School of Business, a ***well-produced video*** *(remember, bad video hurts!)* **increases information retention by 50%** and **speeds-up buying decisions by 72% over a print brochure.** Of the 80% of viewers that have watched a video online, 52% have taken some sort of action. **Prospects are 72% more likely to purchase a product or service when video is used.** Video decreases the time it takes a viewer to reach a buying decision by 70%. **On-line video advertising will grow 72% by 2012 reaching $61 billion.** (Sources: Focus Creative Group, Wharton website, Facebook.com, Linkedin.com, Forrester Research & Nielsen)

Star Power Tip #6

REHEARSE REHEARSE REHEARSE! Know your presentation inside out to overcome jitters. (See Tips #11 and #58 on how to prepare and rehearse a speech.) The better you know it, the less impact nerves will have. Understand that no matter what, a degree of anxiety will always creep in and attempt to derail you. It's normal. Even Oscar winners sometimes throw up before performing! Listen to the *"Core Fundamentals on Handling Nerves"* in the **Unleash Your Star Power!**™ **Home Study Course**. Then practice the exercises, techniques and triggers listed. Learn how to ***turn nerves into a positive*** and ***use them to your advantage*** to improve your performance.

Star Power Tip #7

Create an "Aha Moment" video. What was the life-changing wake-up call that led to where you are today? Describe the pivotal moment. Talk about life before and after. Reveal how the experience fuels you now. Share your goals. For most, **this is a personal mission statement**, where passion lies, simply – why we get up in the morning. It becomes a powerful video to hook viewers! Use it on a website Bio page and in your EPK (*"Electronic Press Kit"*). This also helps prepare the story into *"sound bites"* and *"talking points"* to sprinkle throughout interviews and presentations. So think about it. What was your "Aha Moment?"

Star Power Tip #8

Preparation is truly everything! But remember Murphy's Law. No matter how prepared you are, be ready for anything and keep a sense of humor handy. ***Accidents happen. Use wit to turn it into a plus instead of a negative***. Don't ignore it. Embrace it! Include the audience in the experience because, after all, they are watching and waiting to see how you handle it. This is your chance to be human and endear yourself. One of the best adlibs ever was from my father-in-law, David Niven, during the Oscars when a "streaker" interrupted him on stage. Without missing a beat he said, *"The only laugh that man will ever get in his life is by stripping... and showing his shortcomings."* Brilliant!

Star Power Tip #9

Yikes! Bad first impression? No do-overs here! Make sure you're ready when a media opportunity presents itself. Before facing a camera, doing an interview or giving a presentation, **work with a media coach** to hone your message and performance skills. Olympic athletes work with coaches and so should you. Train with the best, to ensure you are your best. Don't work with someone who was good 10, 5 or even 2 years ago. Trends change and technology evolves quickly. Make sure your coach is active in today's business climate, to give you a competitive edge in current media and marketing strategies. Train, rehearse, and outshine your competition!

Star Power Tip #10

In videos, keep wardrobe simple to showcase your face, not the clothes you're wearing. The correct choice can be dynamite, or at the very least, go pleasantly unnoticed. The wrong choice can be disastrous. Your appearance should be consistent with your message. Business casual is usually best for both men and women. ***Wear something you like that makes you look and feel good***. It's confidence you can't buy. Avoid flashy jewelry (it reflects light), loud prints, white shirts (difficult to get right on-camera), stripes and patterns – anything that will compete for attention. Jangly accessories cause audio problems. Men... unless your target audience is only Execs and CEOs, lose the suit and tie. A jacket and plain shirt (blue is best!) will make you approachable to a wider demographic.

Star Power Tip #11

"Go with the flow and see what happens." NOT! However, never memorize a speech word-for-word either. Memorization keeps you "in your head" and not relating in present time to people with your heart. Instead, ***create a "Mind Map" of your presentation***. Know the open and close, then create bullet points to lead you through the speech. Preparation will carry you through, provided you understand the logic and rehearse the format. When presentation time comes, trust you know your stuff, and that details will be there to pull from as you talk. If done correctly, no two presentations will ever be alike. Be in the moment, delivering it fresh and new, every time.

Star Power Tip #12

Music is a fabulous tool! Use it to handle stress, change your attitude, banish nerves and fire up your energy. Choose a personal *"theme song"* to play when you need to psych yourself up before an important meeting or performance. (Mine is usually the theme from *"Rocky"* – corny, but it works.) Listen in the car, while waiting to go onstage, or before the camera rolls. If using an iPod, wear ear buds and go unnoticed. Practice until you can simply hear it in your mind (without real music) and feel the effect. This is called *"sense memory."* Try it! **Music will keep you focused** and pumped up, so you're ready to kick butt when it's time for *"ACTION!"*

Star Power Tip #13

When doing a TV or radio interview, the more fun you and the other person have, the better response you will get from the audience. ***A sense of "play" is a key ingredient to a good interview*** – it's what hooks viewers and listeners. Sometimes people try so hard to do it right, they become flat and omit personality. Don't try to be perfect. Be authentic and passionate about what you do, and be real. The secret is to truly listen to the other person rather than think too far ahead. If you're not present in the moment, you may miss something. Know your purpose and *"Call-to-Action."* Be ready with personal stories. Have sound bites practiced and ready to insert easily. Then just have fun. Seriously.

Star Power Tip #14

An *"Elevator Speech"* or *"Niche Pitch"* is a brief description of your organization – Who you are, What you do and Why it matters. Practice until it becomes an automatic and natural response to the question: *"What do you do?"* Be prepared with an on-message, concise explanation. This is not your entire story, just a quick taste. **Intrigue them into wanting more.** Focus on who you help and the problems you solve. Keep it simple, convey passion, and hone it to perfection. Have versions ready for 30-seconds (common for networking events), 1-minute and 2-minutes. Be ready to go longer. If you're good, they'll say *"Wow, that's interesting, tell me more!"*

Star Power Tip #15

Shine of any kind is undesirable on-camera. Lights reflect off almost every surface and will be a distraction to video viewers. That includes shiny jewelry, shiny fabrics, shiny faces and shiny bald heads. Even lip gloss and frosted eye shadow can be a problem. Keep everything simple and matte. You want your performance to shine, nothing else! ***Powder is the cure and savior***. Buy a little compact of pressed powder to match your skin tone and apply it liberally throughout the shoot. Powder your face for still-camera photos as well. It reduces shine and flash bulb glare and will ensure you look polished. It's how celebrities make certain they come across their glamorous best on the *"Red Carpet"* and in professional photo shoots.

Star Power Tip #16

Acting coach Milton Katselas was famous for saying, *"Be interested, not interesting."* Wow, that says it all, for any kind of performance. Take the focus off yourself, and concentrate on the audience or other person. **Don't make it all about you. Make it about them**. Think about what you are giving, rather than receiving. An added bonus is you'll be less self-conscious, which will make anxiety and tension dissipate. This also is key when speaking to a video camera. Be specific and decide who you're talking to. Make it personal, not generic. Use someone you know well, like a best friend. Put his or her face in the lens and have a real heart-to-heart chat. Affect them. Change them. GIVE.

Star Power Tip #17

Jump in and start creating *"info"* products. You probably already have material that can easily be repurposed. Got an eBook or blog? If so, turn what you've already written into audio products simply by reading them into a microphone and recording them. Go one step further and create webinars by marrying the audio recording with PowerPoint slides, photos and music. Combine audios or videos with transcriptions to create packages. Or, use written products as the basis for creating *"video tips"* for internet marketing. The possibilities are endless. ***Multipurpose everything!*** Otherwise, it's money left on the table.

Star Power Tip #18

Don't guess. ***Learn exactly what to say and how to say it***. Watch the *"Star Power On-Camera Makeovers"* DVDs included in the ***Unleash Your Star Power!*™ Home Study Course**. Follow amazing transformations as I coach and direct real people on-camera in 15 case studies. Learn how to do a *Video Tip, Welcome Video, Promo Video, Author Video, Sales Video and Opt-in Page Video*. Discover how to: Create your message, Overcome nerves and camera shyness, Make the camera your best friend, Hook people instantly, Work with two people on-camera, Lighten up and lose your inner critic, Hold a book or product, Develop your voice, Introduce yourself the right way, Deliver a *"Call-to-Action,"* Frame shots, Create video testimonials, Use camera and microphone equipment, and much more!

Star Power Tip #19

What happens if you can't read without glasses? Many business execs, politicians, and others in the public eye need them to read the *"teleprompter"* or notes from the podium. It's a lighting disaster waiting to happen. The secret? ***Wear anti-glare lenses.*** A special coating reduces reflection from lights and camera flashes (as well as glare from headlights at night). Affordable? Yes, so think ahead next time you get a new pair. Remember though, it is harder for the viewer to see eyes and read expressions through glasses. It becomes another barrier to overcome when you're trying to make that all-important heart-to-heart connection.

Star Power Tip #20

Create a list of 25 interview questions you prefer to have asked, and then arrange in order of importance. This list will help hone your message and provide the basis for developing your platform. You'll get clear on *"talking points," "sound bites,"* and even *"video tips"* to record later. Have this list (with short, bullet point answers) available to download from the Press section of your website and/or *"EPK"* (Electronic Press Kit). Always send this list of questions in advance to your interviewer to help them do their homework and due diligence. This makes their job easier and will help ensure a good interview that stays on point.

Star Power Tip #21

Nowadays it's possible to **embed audio and video** into a PDF file. Talk about bang-for-your-buck! It creates a million-dollar appearance on a low-budget diet. Use this technology to create expanded, multimedia versions of information products and eBooks. Insert a personal audio or video message into emails, or use video sales letters to completely astound the reader and blow your conversion rate out of the water. Author compilation books embed audios and videos within chapters to create interactive, multimedia versions, expanding hard copy sales into Amazon Best-Sellers. The bonus? Digital multimedia may be instantly downloaded or streamed, which increases profit by saving on hard copy reproduction costs, warehousing, shipping and handling!

Star Power Tip #22

Create your own special phrase or sign-off slogan. Use it at every opportunity in videos, TV interviews, radio shows, audios, speeches, networking events, written materials, business cards, signature lines, and websites. This creates a sense of continuity and branding. It becomes your signature as well as a great *"sound bite."* For instance, mine is: *"Don't settle for less than wonderful in your life. And don't give up five minutes before the miracle!"* That's the core of everything I am. What's your core message?

Star Power Tip #23

Practice your audio technique. Play around reading copy into a tape recorder. Read from a book or magazine article, or jump in and start recording an audio tip or eBook. Play it back. Would you want to listen to you? Work to fine-tune vocal nuances and musicality so you're fun to listen to. Make it a real conversation with your listener, not just dry facts. Don't be afraid to experiment with the colors of your voice. Change up the cadence. Put passion into it. And smile! Although unseen, a smile will still come through in your recording. It creates an instant energy shift the listener will feel and connect with.

Star Power Tip #24

Be careful of hand gestures on-camera. Yes, use body language and hands while talking, to prevent feeling or looking stiff. But don't stab them towards the camera or make gestures too big. The viewer will feel assaulted or, at the very least, distracted. Find out where your *"frame line"* is (the bottom and side borders of the shot), and adjust accordingly. ***Keep body movement and impulses natural, but keep most of your hand movements low, out of frame.*** Some speakers have a hard time adjusting from the big stage to the small screen. Movement must be minimal. Practice in front of the camera until you get it right. Less is more.

Star Power Tip #25

Before any presentation, scout out the room location and space ahead of time in order to rehearse your stage presence. Sneak in for five minutes the night before, or while the room is being set up, or any time during a quick break in the schedule. ***This dry run will help calm nerves*** while you begin to own the space. The point is not to rehearse the script, but to quickly ***feel the stage and work it to your advantage.*** Stand at the podium and visualize the audience. Move around. Test your voice and fill the room without the microphone (in case the sound system fails). Feel the acoustics. Prepare to deliver a dynamite performance!

Star Power Tip #26

When using a video introduction, audio clip or PowerPoint in your presentation, bring two copies with you, one on a CD/DVD and another on a flash drive or laptop. This will make certain at least one format will work with the system being used. Save your PowerPoint in both the latest and older versions of the program, to ensure compatibility. Be ready for Mac or PC. Label everything on the outside cover plus inside on the file itself, because in the chaos of a live event details get forgotten and things misplaced. On arrival, don't just hand it over and assume all will work. Meet the tech person and ***take time to test the mechanics*** to make certain it plays. You don't want to worry about technical difficulties – or be surprised onstage during a live performance. (See Tip #100.)

Star Power Tip #27

Learn to be your own professional spokesperson. Being good on-camera is an art. Look back at yourself on video and ask, *"Would you hire you, or buy from you?"* If not, spend a little time working with a media trainer on-camera to hone your skills. (See Tip #111.) Even hiring a professional videographer doesn't mean you'll come off great, because most don't direct the performance, they only shoot it. They usually sit you on a stool, point the camera at you and say, *"Go."* (Your mind says, *"Go where?!!"*) Don't get caught unprepared. You'll waste money and the inferior performance will hurt rather than help. ***Develop your message, sound bites and camera skills before you need them***. It's the best insurance you can buy.

Star Power Tip #28

Good audio is critical when shooting videos. Most video cameras come with a standard built-in microphone that records everything at one level. This may be adequate in controlled situations, but not outdoors with the wind blowing, or in a noisy room. Voices get lost in the din. The answer is to ***add an external microphone to upgrade sound quality***. What a difference it makes in the end product. Accessories and adapters are available for digital video cameras, such as the Kodak Zi8 and Flip, as well as for Smartphones (iPhone, Android) and for other mobile devices such as the iPad and tablet PCs. Your production value will soar... and so will your image!

Star Power Tip #29

Susan Levin, of Speaker Services in Los Angeles, is an expert on marketing speakers and has a popular speaker listing service. She often gets calls from "newbies" who state they want to be in the speaking biz. When asked for their topic of expertise, a typical comeback is, *"Well, what's the hot topic right now?"* This drives her crazy. Never go into a speech from this standpoint. You must **speak from your own personal experience or passion!** Otherwise, what's the point?

Star Power Tip #30

How do you want to be introduced during an interview or presentation? It's too important to leave to chance. ***Write your "Intro" out ahead of time*** and make it available for easy download in the Meeting Planners and/or Press section of your website and *"Electronic Press Kit."* Don't leave this task to someone else, because no one knows your business better than you. Keep it short, but pithy. Make sure it rolls off the tongue well. Email it beforehand to provide a handy heads-up. Print it out (in extra-large, easy-to-read, **BOLD** type!) to hand to the emcee or person responsible for introducing you. Don't be shy – it's standard procedure. People will appreciate you for making their lives easier.

Star Power Tip #31

Shooting video? Here's how to save hours of editing time. ***Mark your best takes as you shoot them***, because when editing begins, each clip's jpeg image will look exactly alike. You don't want to review hours of recordings to find your favorites. Hollywood films use *"clapboards"* or jot down *"time codes"* to identify each scene. But that's way too time-consuming. Instead, use my secret invention: *"Finger Mark"* your best takes! That means, after a golden take, stop recording. Then immediately put your finger in front of the lens and hit *"record"* again. When you look back, you'll know the takes next to the "finger" are your best ones!

Star Power Tip #32

One of the most important aspects on a set is knowing how to **hit your mark**. A mark is the place on the floor where you must stand, or the exact spot you must hit when bringing a book or product up into the shot. It's critical for *"focus"* and shot composition. If you have a director, he'll guide you. But if on your own, watch playback on a monitor to guide yourself. Determine the perfect placement in the frame and set your mark. Once you've set it, hit it every time. To make a floor mark visible, use tape ("X" marks the spot). If walking into the shot, my favorite trick is to use a *"sandbag"* as a mark. Simply feel it against the foot and land perfectly, without looking down to find it.

Star Power Tip #33

The sound and strength of your voice is one of the most important components of public speaking. It will influence the impact of your message, and possibly make or break the success of your speech, TV appearance, teleseminar or audio product. Bob Corff, Celebrity Voice Coach to the Stars says, *"Your voice is the autobiography of your soul."* What does yours say about you? If you don't have a great voice yet, start developing one now! It's vital to *learn the basics of placement, support and tone*. Discover exercises and techniques to help turn your voice into a powerful instrument in the *Unleash Your Star Power!*™ **Home Study Course**. Then, if the sound system goes out (it happens!) you'll still be able to hit the back row without a microphone, just like actors do in the theater.

Star Power Tip #34

Think video rather than text. Look around for photo ops that inspire quick, on-location videos. It's your own Reality TV. Almost anything can be turned into a clever message, short teaching bit or *"man-on-the-street"* interview setup. Use a webcam at the office, or be ready to pull out your pocket camera or Smartphone when you see something that might work. Create fun little messages for email, ezines or newsletters, and Facebook and other social media sites. Consider sending a short video email to clients rather than a written one. It makes a very personal thank you after a great meeting!

Star Power Tip #35

Microphone Secrets: Whether using a podium *"mic"* or a stand-up microphone, adjust the height and positioning before starting. You don't want to fight it throughout your presentation. Ask for help and feedback, if needed. Do a *"sound check"* to test levels before you begin speaking by scratching the mic with a fingernail to see if it's turned on. This is less obtrusive than saying *"testing"* or *"check."* If using a handheld microphone, hold it a few inches away from, and just below, the mouth. Never breathe directly into it. Exhaling will cause wind sound effects and annoying pops. Wear a *"lavaliere"* microphone clipped to your shirt for hands-free convenience. Warning: You'll never know for sure when your mic is *"hot"* (turned on) so be careful of comments you want to keep off the record!

Star Power Tip #36

Think like a Producer and **set up the shot, lighting and situation to best advantage**. If shooting outside, don't shoot in bright overhead sunlight because it's too harsh. It causes squinting, creates ugly shadows and accentuates bags under eyes. Find shade or a tree to stand under to diffuse the light and make it flattering. A cloudy day makes a beautiful *"light filter."* Consider the background too. If it's too bright, or if shooting into a light source, the camera will try to adjust and the image will be too dark. Check the monitor and playback each time you move the camera or set up a new shot. Make sure all looks good and is framed correctly. Adjust everything until you like what you see. Then... *"roll camera!"*

Star Power Tip #37

Do your homework and ***tailor your presentation to the audience you will be speaking to***. Even if recycling the same basic speech or PowerPoint, making small, minor adjustments for each group will keep it new and fresh and customized. This pays off substantially with better audience retention and happy clients. When hired to speak, ask the meeting planner or person in charge for details about the group or company, including specifics and stories you can use about their people, goals or plans. Or heck, do a little online research – it's worth the effort.

Star Power Tip #38

On the set before shooting a TV interview, create an opportunity to connect with the host or interviewer in a personal way. If it's your show, make your guest comfortable and do a little bonding. Find something you have in common and **establish a quick relationship**, because it will come across on-camera. A word of caution though. Don't talk in detail about the interview subject matter, except to get a heads-up on planned questions and the show format. (See Tip #78.) Keep the rest of it fresh and surprising. It's always better the first time through, so save it for the camera.

Star Power Tip #39

There's a trick to holding products correctly on-camera. It's why professional actors and hand models are paid the big bucks. Aesthetics matter. ***Practice in a mirror*** so the item looks good in your hands. Don't clutch it with a death grip! Relax elbows, wrists and fingers. Check your manicure in case of close-ups. Avoid covering the print or title, and hold it in a way that shows you actually like it. (We call it *"romancing the product."*) Yes, even a box of breakfast cereal can be sexy! Body language is important. Rehearse bringing it up and down naturally and gracefully. Study commercials and mimic techniques. Notice timing and small details. Go to QVC or HSN for great examples. (See Tip #109 for technical details on holding products.)

Star Power Tip #40

Quick tips for Authors: ***Create a video to promote your book*** and include it on your website and *"EPK"* (Electronic Press Kit). Tell the viewer what problems the book solves and the benefits they'll get from reading it, instead of merely talking about yourself. Show the book at some point, as a natural extension of the conversation you're having with the camera. (Check Tip #39.) Add personality! Be fun to watch, especially if you want a shot at getting national publicity through big-time media outlets. It's highly competitive out there. ***What's your unique hook? What sets you apart?*** Producers are looking for "remarkable" interview guests, so think *"Show Business."* Show them you know how to entertain the troops.

Star Power Tip #41

Be respectful of time schedules and restrictions! Speakers are given a certain amount of time to present, yet so many disregard parameters and run over. This is the ultimate in disrespect and self-importance, and can throw off the event's entire schedule. If other speakers are set to follow, they may be forced to take time-cuts to compensate. ***Be a team player.*** Word gets around. Believe me, a "Diva Attitude" will ensure you don't get booked again.

Star Power Tip #42

Nobody likes how he or she looks or sounds the first time they watch themselves on-camera... ever! ***Get the critic off your shoulder*** and lighten up***.*** No one is born knowing how to do this. It's all technique, which you will learn. And here's a secret. After viewing playback several times, you'll forget it's you and see it objectively in the third person. While watching, pick out what you did right and build on that in each consecutive performance. Then marvel at how far you've come. Celebrating "wins" will make them concrete, and you will get better and better each time.

Star Power Tip #43

Before any performance, ***exercise your mouth and tongue*** to release tension and warm up. Stress can cause facial muscles to tighten and vocalizations to freeze up. Grab the end of your tongue in your fingers and say the ABCs, working your mouth as much as you can to over-enunciate. Really stretch the face and lips. Take your hand away and be surprised at how much clearer you can speak and pronounce words. Find more voice exercises in the ***Unleash Your Star Power!***™ **Home Study Course**. Don't be shy about using these methods on the set. Crews are used to performers warming up their instruments (mind, voice and body). They will respect you for doing whatever it takes to ensure the best possible performance.

Star Power Tip #44

If you are being recorded, always request a copy. Write it into your contract. Get video or audio copies of everything you do, including taped presentations, TV appearances, radio interviews, videos, teleseminars and webinars. Later, use short clips of these when putting together a demo or promo reel. It's important to **have tape on yourself** because people want to see what you've already done, and how well you come across – before they book you. Later if you decide to repurpose that great recording into a CD, or transcribe it into an eBook, be sure to have permission first. Even though it's YOUR performance and/or intellectual property, you may not have rights to reuse or resell it. It's another thing to negotiate.

Star Power Tip #45

When shooting videos, keep the camera rolling through every take. You never know when you'll hit the golden one. Nobody has to know how many takes it took to get there – just delete everything else. When shooting a movie or TV show, I always ask to keep the camera rolling and *"rehearse on tape."* **First takes are often best** because that's when you get happy accidents. After awhile you start to get stale. If so, do whatever it takes to get fresh again. Don't echo or "robot" what you've already done. Switch it up. Think out of the box. Try something different in the next take. Do something absurd to shake things up and change the pattern. Surprise yourself back to "first take magic!"

Star Power Tip #46

Speaking is always a performance! However, few people fully utilize key acting skills and an entertainer's perspective in their presentations. Actors know the importance of setting the stage, using vocal nuances, creating characters, and fully utilizing their tool box to effectively elicit desired emotions and responses in the audience. Tools and techniques include *"improvisation,"* timing, lighting, dramatic staging, *"props,"* wardrobe, body language, listening skills, emotional availability, personal stories, creating a dynamic open and close, *"The Moment Before," "sense memory,"* etc. By using simple acting skills, you will dramatically increase your effectiveness and make yourself memorable. Never underestimate the value of entertainment. Make your presentation Oscar-worthy!

Star Power Tip #47

A fabulous way to utilize video is on the *"FAQ"* (Frequently Asked Questions) page of your website. **Create questions** you think clients might ask about your business, products and services. Then **answer with "talking head" video clips** (that means you talking to the camera) posted under the question. You might want to incorporate "how-to" demonstrations, troubleshooting tips, video tutorials, before and after stories, guest interviews and testimonials. Some people would rather read than watch a video, so consider transcribing the "answer" videos into text, and post on the page as well. People physically take in, process and remember information differently. Having both versions available covers two learning modalities.

Star Power Tip #48

Don't wait for PERFECT before going on-camera. I can't tell you how many times I've heard people say they need a marketing or promotional video, and want to shoot with me in my studio, but... they must lose ten pounds first. Some people are still waiting two years later. Hey, we all want to look good, but remember it's a process. ***"Perfect" is paralyzing.*** Don't wait – get something you can use now, and then build on it.

Star Power Tip #49

Lighting on every stage is different. Before speaking, have someone sit in the audience to tell you where the lights hit best. Too many speakers omit this. It won't matter how great you are on stage if people can't see you. It's hard to judge a spotlight when standing in it, so **feedback is important**. Check for microphone shadows at the podium too. Walk the entire stage, and if warranted, the audience area. Sometimes going into the audience backfires. If people up front lose your face for very long, you lose them. Map out where to stand and how to turn, to ensure you will be seen clearly by everyone.

Star Power Tip #50

Don't let your face fade into the background! Even if you never wear makeup, you might have to wear a smidgen to **make sure you "pop" on-camera**. Men and women alike, especially blondes, wash out under the lights. Eyes truly are the window to the soul, so enhance them if necessary. If adding foundation or "tan" to the face, apply it also to other exposed body parts, like neck, backs of hands, arms and bare legs. Ensure all visible skin matches. When holding *"props,"* white hands stick out like a sore thumb. For an important photo or video shoot, hire a professional makeup and hair person to do it right. The bonus? D.I.Y. Watch how they do it, so next time you can do it yourself.

Star Power Tip #51

Use your personal "Before and After" story. James Malinchak calls it your *"Mess to Success."* These are the embarrassing photos or stories from nerdy high school days or other challenging periods. It will help the audience connect to you as a real person. We all have them. I use my dreaded, fat-girl adolescent photos – the ones I quake at sharing. James uses photos from his *"Miami Vice"* fad days. **Resurrect old photos and stories of yourself** too, in order to disclose your "Before" in all its glory. This will make your "After" reveal much more powerful.

Star Power Tip #52

Wonder what color to wear on-camera? Choose something that will **coordinate with your branding and publicity materials**. If planning to use the video on your website, the priority is to wear what looks good without clashing with the color scheme. It doesn't have to be an exact match – but carry out the style and theme. Here are industry rules on color: The camera loves blue the best, and generally has trouble with red, white and black. Red tends to *"bleed."* Avoid white because the camera will try to *"white balance,"* and the look of your face will suffer during the adjustment. Black sometimes looks like a black hole on camera and can suck the energy out of a shot. It takes lighting and exposure expertise to make these colors work. If you have it, great! If not, play it safe.

Star Power Tip #53

Pick up a pack of clothespins and stash them in your video kit. They're handy for a lot of things. Blouse too big? Use one behind your back as an instant tailoring tool to make wardrobe fit better. Use them to attach diffusion paper onto a hot studio light, hold a microphone cord out of the way, or clasp notes together in a pinch. All these years on film sets I've heard big, brawny *"grips"* and *"gaffers"* yelling, *"Get me a C-47!"* Turns out they were talking about plain, ordinary clothespins! Crew members keep them clipped to utility belts, looking like gunslingers. Hence, they're also called *"bullets."* A real, behind-the-scenes Hollywood secret, ***clothespins will become your go-to quick fix***.

Star Power Tip #54

When people land on your website you need to **capture contact information**. I recommend offering three free gifts as an incentive to opt in or sign up. For example, offer any combination of these: Top 5 Tips, eBook, special report, audio, webinar, video, online newsletter or ezine, ticket to a seminar, free consultation, discounted products or services, etc. Stay away from anything requiring snail mail. Digital delivery is best, as it can be set up for automatic, instant downloading which avoids shipping and handling on your part. Make sure to give away some of your best stuff without compromising intellectual secrets. Prove the value! Promise "amazing" and then over-deliver. If they like what they see and hear, they'll tell their friends and come back for more.

Star Power Tip #55

Start now to **begin building a series of** "**Video Tips**." (Set a long term goal of at least thirty.) Once created, this little goldmine of information will help establish you as the Celebrity Expert in your niche. Video ranks higher on search engines than text, so it's easy to rise quickly if *"Search Engine Optimization"* is done effectively. Then take it further. Repurpose and creatively bundle your treasures into information products and sell away! (See Tip #17.) Value added supports a higher price point at the sales counter. Turn the videos into a DVD series or develop an online eCourse. Transcribe them (a single 3-minute video becomes approximately a 400-word article) and repurpose into eBooks, reports, etc... and quite possibly, the foundation for your very own *"Home Study System."*

Star Power Tip #56

Want to be great at interviews? Here's how Oprah defined it. She said, *"Jon Stewart is a great television guest,"* which is why she had him on her show many times. *"He knows and understands television as well as timing. He knows how to say something poignant, direct and funny in a short amount of time. It's a dance. He understands the dance and he comes to play."* Take your cue from the masters. **Come to dance and come to play.**

Star Power Tip #57

On the day of your presentation, get to the event room well ahead of time. (Yes, this is worth repeating.) Make sure you have everything on your check list, and that technical and electrical connections are working. Set up the space and podium with necessities: water, *"props,"* PowerPoint remote and your speech or notes. Then be vigilant, because something might get rearranged or the speaker ahead of you may accidentally grab your papers or other items when leaving the stage. Recently I witnessed a speaker walk on stage to discover his laptop (and entire presentation) was missing. Not fun, especially in front of 200 people. ***Carry a backup of everything vital***, just in case.

Star Power Tip #58

An effective way to rehearse a presentation is to go over it the last thing before falling asleep. During the night the subconscious works on it, and when you awaken, it will be more firmly implanted in your mind. Another way is to record it on a tape recorder and play it in the background. Listen while driving, doing tasks at your desk or even as you're waiting in line. ***Get very clear on the open, close, outline and bullet points***. Remember though! The goal is not to memorize it exactly, but to merely walk through it in your head. And here's an added benefit. If you're not tied to a set script it's easy to adjust speech length, even last minute, simply by adding or deleting a bullet point or two.

Star Power Tip #59

Plug your website and contact details into every media opportunity. Identify yourself clearly so it's easy for people to locate you for follow-up. In videos, add it to end credits. For interviews and appearances, ask editors, hosts and producers to include your contact info on all promo materials, with direct links to your website from theirs. If asking a question from the audience (in person or on a teleseminar line), state your name, website, city of residence, and what you do... before proceeding. If questionable, spell the website URL – it's important. You never know who is in the room, or who may see or hear the recording later. It could bring a new customer!

Star Power Tip #60

When delivering a niche pitch at a networking event, don't be afraid to be dramatic and different. Never limit the moment to name, company and service. BORING! Don't play safe because you'll sound like everyone else. Even if you only have 30 seconds, stand out! It's vital to **give a glimpse of your personality** and catch the group's attention. Try something new. Then, when something garners positive feedback, and people offer their business cards because of it, use it again the next time. It's a keeper!

Star Power Tip #61

Appearance is important – even on the radio. So SMILE! It will supercharge you and your performance, and travel straight to the core of the listener. People sense it even when unseen. Test this yourself. Practice reading *"copy"* into a tape recorder. Rehearse with a smile, then without. Hear and feel the instant energy change. Wardrobe is also essential. Don't sit in pajamas for an important audio recording or interview, even if no one is watching. Spruce up and wear what makes you feel powerful. It will make a huge difference in self-confidence and bump your performance to the next level.

Star Power Tip #62

When introducing yourself in a video, **look into the camera and speak as if greeting your best friend**. Don't say: *"Hello, my name is..."* unless you're an unusually formal person. It keeps the viewer at a distance. Instead give a genuine "it's great to see you" smile and say, *"Hi, I'm..."* because it's much more friendly and personal. Your goal is to be warm and approachable, to come across as someone the viewer wants to spend time with. So, be authentic in your performance, **tap into the excitement about what you're sharing, and... enjoy yourself!** When you have fun, so do we! Reveal your heart, sense of humor and unique personality. Don't try to be a carbon copy of anyone else. You lose us the moment you put on "fake." We want to be captivated by YOU, charming quirks and all!

Star Power Tip #63

Want to be memorable? Here's an easy formula I learned from my mentor, Jack Barnard, who I call the Wizard of Oz for Speakers. He says, *"Remember the FOUR Es. To give your audience a true EXPERIENCE, you must EDUCATE, ENGAGE and ENTERTAIN. Educate in order to impart information. Engage the audience. And don't forget to add the magic ingredient – Entertainment."* He's right. The experience you give them and the emotional journey you take them on is more important than facts and figures. **They won't remember exactly what you said, but they'll remember how you made them feel**.

Star Power Tip #64

When shooting a video for the internet, it will most likely be shot from the waist up (*"medium shot"*), bust up (*"medium close-up"*) or shoulders up (*"close-up"*). Stay away from wide shots, as details will get lost on the small computer screen. Tight shots create intimacy and a personal connection. As you talk to camera, **speak intimately** as if the viewer is about 24 inches away. Even if the camera is across the room, don't try to project your voice to reach it. The microphone will pick up everything, even a whisper. Keep energy up, but don't push it. Men especially, if not careful, can come across as too loud or aggressive on-camera. Don't bombard or shoo people away. Instead, be gentle and vulnerable to draw people close. Speak from your heart and **invite the viewer in**.

Star Power Tip #65

The moment before you speak is the most important of all. In fact, there's an actor's term coined by the famous acting coach, Stanislavsky, called *"The Moment Before."* It's important because it fuels every other moment of your performance. Make certain to get into the right frame of mind before speaking the first word. To psych yourself up, use exercises and triggers such as those found in the ***Unleash Your Star Power!*™ Home Study Course**. Without the "juice" going into your presentation, you could fall flat and run out of steam. Start right out of the box at an emotional "10" and it will carry you to the finish.

Star Power Tip #66

Have doubles of video and audio equipment ready, especially if it's an important session or interview. There's nothing worse than canceling everything and everyone because of technical difficulties. Make sure you **know how to troubleshoot**, or have someone with expertise available on speed dial. Keep camera and microphone instruction manuals in your bag for easy reference. Have backups of backups. Here's a partial list of extras to have nearby: batteries, microphones, cables, adapters, light bulbs, even an extra camera if you have that luxury.

Star Power Tip #67

When doing a webinar or teleseminar, ***hire a technical "wingman"*** so you can focus on your extraordinary presentation. Concentrate solely on what you're saying and the performance. If distracted by technical details, you won't be fully present or relate as well to your audience. Your wingman should do all the technical stuff, including starting the recording (believe it or not, this is something that's easy to forget!), interacting with attendees and guests on procedural issues, troubleshooting, routing questions to you, etc. Flying solo is risky.

Star Power Tip #68

Be proactive against sound problems. If wearing a *"lav mic"* (lavaliere microphone), test out fabric and wardrobe before recording begins, to prevent rustling noises. If questionable, change clothing. Use a *"windscreen"* over the top of the mic, especially when shooting outdoors, to buffer wind noise and breath sounds. If recording audio indoors, do your best to create a *"sound booth"* area. Find a quiet corner away from windows (to shut out noise from jets, cars and barking dogs) and set up your mic on a stable desk, about 4-6 inches from your mouth. Use a windscreen to prevent pops. Keep in mind **the microphone picks up everything**, including a growling stomach. If you're hungry, it will provide an audible sound track that's extremely hard to remove. Keep nuts or energy snacks within easy reach.

Star Power Tip #69

Most speakers believe they must deliver a *"monologue."* BORING. Don't merely impart information or speak <u>at</u> the audience. Make them part of the process. Create a *"dialogue,"* whether they are actually talking back or not. This holds true when talking to a camera lens, recording an audio, doing a radio show, or presenting to a live group. It's basic communication. Send out your message. Let it land. Watch the reaction (or imagine it if speaking to a camera or microphone), absorb it, and allow it to affect the delivery of your next thought. Give and receive moment to moment, sharing the experience full circle. **Take your cue off the audience** and turn your presentation into a living, breathing, intriguing tango.

Star Power Tip #70

Music adds tremendous production value to audio and video recordings, elevating their worth. Warning: Don't just use a favorite song from your iPod – it's more than likely illegal. Check out copyright laws and choose or purchase accordingly. ***Search for royalty free music*** and spend time surfing sites. You'll be surprised at how much is available. Find something you like, purchase the rights to use it and download directly from the website. Try different music themes and have fun selecting the perfect tune to reflect the right energy or mood of the project.

Star Power Tip #71

You booked a television interview? Congrats! Now get busy. Be über-prepared. Research your host, the show, the station and demographics to provide confidence and insider details. Talk to the segment producer about the purpose of the interview and be clear on goals and objectives. Submit your Bio, Intro and 25 Questions. (See Tip #20.) Discuss wardrobe. (See Tip #94.) Ask about hair and makeup – is it provided, or are you responsible? Unless told otherwise, arrive *"camera ready"* with normal makeup and hair and let them fine-tune. Bring several wardrobe choices. Find out if *"Green Screen"* will be used. If so, adjust accordingly. (See Tip #74.) Get driving directions, print them out, and arrive early so you don't stress – and they don't panic!

Star Power Tip #72

Speakers, it's important to have video of your presentation(s) on your website and *"EPK"* (Electronic Press Kit). A great *"Video Demo"* will make you money and dramatically increase speaking fees. **Meeting planners want to see you in action** in front of a live group, and often all they go by is what they see in your demo reel. It's your *"commercial."* Make it dynamic and professional! Include clips from the presentation, audience reaction shots, testimonials, music and *"voice-over."* It's worth the investment to hire a crew to film and edit, so you look and sound like a pro. Find out more about Video Demo group shooting days, Workshops, 3-Day Boot Camps, and custom video production services (including personal coaching & directing) at **www.UnleashYourStarPower.com**.

Star Power Tip #73

Glasses? Lose them on-camera if feasible, especially if using lighting equipment. ***Lights glare off lenses*** with head movement. It's nearly impossible to avoid unless lenses are anti-glare. (See Tip #19.) Frames can also cause reflection problems. If worn in spite of these challenges, ***play around with angles***. Tip glasses up slightly off the ears to angle lenses down and away from lights. Also try moving them down the nose and/or tilting your head downward. Be aware though that restricting head movement also restricts natural body movement, which may hurt your performance. Do your best to manage an imperfect situation. Or better yet... take them off and go naked!

Star Power Tip #74

Green Screen: (aka *"Chroma Key"*) A process where subjects are shot in front of a colored backdrop. The backdrop is used as a *"key"* then replaced with another image (video clip, graphic or still photo) either in real-time, as with TV weather presenters, or most often afterwards in post-production. Today it's easy and relatively inexpensive to use this technology in a home studio. Go online and research kits that include background and lights, and find online tutorials for proper lighting, shooting and editing. If utilizing *"Green Screen,"* **avoid wearing green** or you will partially disappear on camera and the background will show through. It can also be problematic for green-eyed people.

Star Power Tip #75

After 25 years in show business, I still suffer anxiety watching myself in a new TV or movie role. At first all I see are personal flaws and imperfections. But something happens part way through. Objectivity clicks in and I watch as if it were someone else, not me. I concentrate on the performance itself. *"Now that was a good moment. So was that. Well, maybe I could have done better on that line... but yes, that was a good choice right there!"* Borrow this technique. Study the "game" film. ***Review, evaluate and improve.*** It's a Champion mindset.

Star Power Tip #76

Most of the work you'll do hosting your own radio or TV show will relate to booking guests. People will say yes, and unfortunately, fail on the follow-through. ***Pre-produce your guests*** before inking them in to the schedule. Don't book anyone until all requirements and submissions are met. Must-haves include photo, website, bio, intro and their list of 25 Questions. (Check Tip #20.) You want guests who respect and value your time and the opportunity. Odds are a flaky prospect will become a flaky interview.

Star Power Tip #77

Makeup for men: Less is more, and basic translucent powder is probably all that's needed. ***Powder is crucial on faces and receding hairlines*** because hot lights (and stress) will make you perspire and look shiny. However, if skin is blotchy or red, or there are noticeable dark circles that lighting can't hide, you may need more than powder to even out skin tones and give a healthy glow. Men with dark beard lines or oily skin are not flattered by the camera – but it's an easy fix. Out of your territory here? Get advice from a professional or go to a department store and ask someone at the counter for help with products and application tips. On shoot day, shave at least an hour before camera time to prevent irritation, making sure to groom ear and nose hair if necessary.

Star Power Tip #78

Time flies in a TV or radio situation so don't waste it. You are there to do business, not good ol' jawboning with the other person. ***Stay on purpose!*** Go over details and technical structure beforehand to make every moment count. Get clear on timing. Know the format for *"intro"* and *"outro"* cues and commercial breaks. If on a TV set, ask about *"camera eyeline"* (where to look). Find out what questions you'll be asked in order to plan your thought structure in advance. Discuss your *"Call-to-Action,"* asking when and how it will be mentioned. (Will they bring it up, or is it up to you?) When the session starts, be aware of the clock and ***make sure to get everything in.*** Interviews can end abruptly, so don't wait until the last minute. You may be S.O.L.

Star Power Tip #79

While facing an audience, really look at them. People sometimes advise to stare above their heads, or imagine them without clothes. Well, that's silly! How can you connect and have an impact that way? Instead, make direct eye contact and choose people to land on. While speaking, continually take the temperature of audience members. Effect them, let them effect you. Your performance will have a true heart and soul connection and each will feel you are speaking to them personally. This also helps with nerves, because you'll see them as real people instead of a big blur. They will become allies, not adversaries.

Star Power Tip #80

Videos shot from the waist up? What you wear on the bottom isn't critical as long as it doesn't show in the frame. (You'd be surprised what news anchors wear behind the desk.) If shooting a series of videos, have several tops ready and switch them out as you go. Add or remove a jacket. Change your blouse or shirt. Vary jewelry. Drape a scarf. Add a pop of color. Pull your hair back. ***Wardrobe and hairstyles will help distinguish one video from another***. This gives the illusion you didn't shoot everything the same day... even if you did!

Star Power Tip #81

Do a strategic analysis to **determine your best** "**keywords**" (words or phrases which prospects might type into a search engine) and **plan video content around them**. Don't start shooting videos based on what you only assume people want, as most do. Research to laser-focus efforts and ultimately, results. Later incorporate keywords into video titles to maximize *"Search Engine Optimization."* If uploading video to sites like You Tube, learn how to most effectively complete the description area. This process helps boost you in search engines and will drive traffic to your website. When you hit first-page ranking, you become King of the Hill and the Go-to Expert in your category.

Star Power Tip #82

For any kind of media presentation, research and *mirror the style and unique qualities of your target audience* so you can best connect with them. Be authentic while portraying the image, role or personality traits needed to enhance a mutual relationship. This will cue wardrobe selections, body language, makeup, jewelry, voice placement, personal stories, etc. If in Texas, wear boots and a cowboy hat, y'all.

Star Power Tip #83

Makeup for women: Treat yourself and invest in the services of a professional makeup and hair person who specializes in camera work. Professional videos call for quality. It's money well spent to worry less about looks and more about performance. Talk about building confidence! If doing it yourself, *keep it simple but effective*, much like your normal street makeup. Don't be heavy-handed with lipstick, blush, eyeliner or bright-colored eye shadow. Today's High Definition cameras are hypersensitive and amplify every detail. Remember to powder your face during the shoot to keep shine-free. Have hair spray handy for stray hairs, which can be very noticeable against the background. Keep a mirror close by for touchups.

Star Power Tip #84

When wearing a *"lavaliere"* microphone, ***worry more about getting good sound than trying to hide the mic***. Even Oprah let her *"lav mic"* be visible. It's the best way to ensure clean audio. Clip it to your lapel securely so it won't slip out of place, and hide the wire inside clothing. Find a spot where the mic won't rub on wardrobe, jewelry or hair, or be bumped by hand gestures. Put on headphones and move body and arms around to test and listen for fabric rustle. If necessary, reset the mic or change clothes to keep sound clean. Attach the battery pack to a belt or waistband, or tuck inside a pocket. Use a *"C-47"* to clip the wire to the back of your shirt, out of the way. (Check Tip #53.) Be careful not to touch the microphone or step on the cable while recording, which will cause audio bumps.

Star Power Tip #85

Chaos on the set? Time is money, and you'll have dozens of people scurrying back and forth on stage around you, preparing for the shot. ***Don't let the stress get to you.*** Use the adrenalin to fuel your performance instead of letting it shut you down. Be open and present. Talk to others on the set, relate to people and keep a sense of play going. When you relax and start having fun, those around you will too. It's contagious. It dissipates the tension and builds a team mindset. And that is when magic happens!

Star Power Tip #86

A good video marketing campaign should utilize three types of videos: *Professional videos, webcam videos, and Smartphone or pocket camera videos* (like the Kodak Zi8 or Flip camera) for fun moments. They all have their place. But it's essential to **use only professional quality videos on the main pages of your website**. Especially critical are welcome, sales and landing pages. These are the first images people will judge you by. If the videos don't look professional, you won't look or sound professional either, no matter how good you are in your business. ***A poorly produced video will slash the perceived value of your product or service.***

Star Power Tip #87

For radio interviews, call from a landline, never a cell. You want the best reception possible. No speaker phones either, for the same reason, as voice quality will suffer. Here's a professional tip to optimize sound over a telephone line: ***Treat the phone handset like a microphone***. Don't speak directly into it as normal. Rather, lower the mouthpiece to chin level and ***speak above it, not into it***. This will ensure the audio doesn't pick up breathing noises or "popping" sounds from consonants. YOU might not hear it while on the call itself, but the audience will – and it will be very evident in the recording later.

Star Power Tip #88

The internet levels the playing field. If done correctly, it allows you to compete with the Big Dogs. Ineffectively, you'll never be a contender. Get the biggest bang for the buck by maximizing everything across multiple platforms. *"Social Networking"* and *"Search Engine Optimization"* of your website, videos, articles and blogs are vital to growing your presence. This used to be pretty straight-forward. But nowadays it's more complicated and time consuming to do it right, with new rules and regulations. Doing it wrong can even red-flag and ban your site! For maximum, worry-free results, use time and money wisely and **hire an expert who is up on current tricks, trends and strategies** to do it for you. The return is well worth the investment, and you can concentrate on what you do best.

Star Power Tip #89

Pre-planning will help **avoid noise distractions** when doing a live radio interview, teleseminar or webinar. It's hard to concentrate on content in a chaotic environment. Be proactive and head off problems before they occur. This includes kids, cell phones, barking dogs, text messages, TV, alarm clocks, squeaky chairs, snoring spouses, doorbells, dishwashers, crazy neighbors, running water and flushing toilets. **Remember... any noise you hear will be going out live over the air**. If something does go wrong, be speedy with the *"mute"* button if necessary. Monitor the conversation on speaker to stay mentally connected while you correct the issue, then hit *"unmute"* ASAP and jump right back in without missing a beat. Whew!

Star Power Tip #90

Be on the lookout to **create and capture photo ops** and testimonials, any time and anywhere. Use a pocket camera or Smartphone to record instant video gems for Facebook, You Tube, blogs and email. However, *"production values"* still count, even in a spur-of-the-moment situation. Take an extra minute to figure out the shot. Be aware of lighting, background, shot composition and shiny noses. Keep powder handy for yourself and any other on-camera subjects. When ready, *"roll camera,"* then playback immediately to make sure you got the shot. If needed, do additional takes. Perhaps you need to hone your *"stand up"* wording or change the camera angle. When satisfied, get signed talent releases from each person who appears on-camera, even in the background. (Check Tip #101.)

Star Power Tip #91

How's your memory? When working from a prepared script with two or more people, you may be forced to memorize multiple pages. If so, use this trick from my soap opera days, when I had countless pages of dialogue to learn. Get a tape recorder and record all lines of the script except yours, leaving blank pauses for your lines as you say them silently in your head. During playback, speak your lines aloud at the appropriate moment and rehearse the scene. You'll learn it quickly by using audio cues instead of just trying to remember text on a page. Play this recording just before sleep at night, and get ready to be pleasantly surprised when you wake up with your lines down.

Star Power Tip #92

Nothing's worse than returning from a great video recording session only to discover it is unusable due to a technical problem. Don't be shocked when you get home. ***Do video playback check-ins*** constantly, especially each time you move a light or change a camera angle. Check for things like framing, lighting, clarity, focus, background, color and sound. Make sure lights and light stands, camera equipment, cables, reflections, scripts, *"looky-loos"* at the location, coffee cups, water bottles, hair spray, makeup and other unwanted items stay out of the shot. Surprises happen even on big budget movie sets. There's only so much that can be fixed in editing.

Star Power Tip #93

Heavy makeup? Eeeww! We live in the age of Reality TV and savvy viewers. Apply too much thick makeup and the magic of HD (High Definition) will reveal your secret in a heartbeat. You're trying too hard. ***Makeup is an element that is best when it goes unnoticed***. Realize nobody ever likes how he or she looks. Don't over think and try not to overcorrect. People want to see the real you, not your makeup. On the other hand, if there truly is a flaw that needs concealing, ask a professional makeup artist for advice on how to camouflage scars, blemishes, discolorations, and dark circles.

Star Power Tip #94

When sharing camera time, as in a TV studio interview, be flexible and **coordinate wardrobe items with everyone involved**. Talk to the producer ahead of time for suggestions. Ask about the background color of the set. You don't want clothing to blend in and make you invisible. Find out if *"Green Screen"* will be used, and if so, avoid anything green. (See Tip #74.) On shoot day, bring a few changes to provide options. Be willing to compromise – it's not all about you. You may love your blue suit, but if the other person is wearing the same color, you may have to change. Also, it gets hot under studio lights. Dress for the heat, but bring a jacket or sweater to compensate for air-conditioning before you go on. Consider dress shields if you perspire easily.

Star Power Tip #95

Don't over-rehearse. Trying to be perfect is not the goal, and may backfire. Rehearse too much to get it just right, and freshness goes down the drain. Try to time your peak for when the camera is rolling. Otherwise, it will be an empty echo of a magic moment gone by. If only the camera had been recording then! Digital cameras have changed everything. It's not like the old days when film was expensive. Today on the set we hear, *"Tape is cheap, let it roll." **Record everything**,* including your first takes, and sort it out later.

Star Power Tip #96

What's the right length for a video? It varies. A welcome video on your website can be fairly short, about 1 to 1-1/2 minutes long. Just long enough for people to meet you, find you charming and credible, and hear your pitch. Most marketing videos for the internet and You Tube should be 2-1/2 to 3 minutes in length. The cool thing about a 3-minute video is that when transcribed, it makes about a 400-word article (the perfect length to submit to search engines). Anything longer than 4 minutes is pushing it, and you're probably rambling. Get concise or split one long video into several shorter, dynamic ones. And remember... today's viewer has a short attention span, so you've always gotta hook 'em in the first 10 seconds!

Star Power Tip #97

Be prepared to ***troubleshoot audio problems*** on the spot. A sign of a dying battery is a slight buzz in the headphones, which will sound even worse during editing. Bring extra batteries for the microphone to be replaced quickly if needed. Crossed wires and cables can cause buzzing too. Trace backward to detangle and if still a problem, test to see if one has gone bad. If so, switch it out. Rarely, random radio signals can also cause audio interference. There's not much to do except move the *"shoot"* to another location. Sometimes humming from overhead lights, refrigerators or air conditioning can be heard in the background. It will probably sound worse in editing. If necessary, turn off lights or the A/C, and pull the plug on the fridge while shooting. Just remember to plug it back in afterward.

Star Power Tip #98

First impressions mean everything – so make yours fabulous! ***Invest in a professional studio shoot***. Great welcome and sales videos aren't shot in the backyard. Look and sound your best, as you have only seconds to hook and connect with the viewer. Be unique, inject a sense of humor and speak with passion and expertise. Come across as professional and personal. And don't forget your *"Call-to-Action!"* Out of your element? Don't worry. Learn what to say, including preparation and performance secrets, in the **Unleash Your Star Power!™ Home Study Course**. Then on shoot day, be thrilled with your confidence level and astonished at your new, professional image. Or better yet, come to my studio and let me coach and direct you in person! (See Tip #111).

Star Power Tip #99

Technology. You don't have to leave your driveway to do a radio show. Calling from home? Start getting ready at least 30 minutes before the scheduled interview. ***Set yourself up for success by preparing the space to be an efficient "Studio Control Room."*** Use a landline and disable call-waiting, so incoming calls won't disturb the session. Be familiar with using the phone handset as a microphone. (See Tip #87.) Turn off the cell and close the door and window. (Leaf blowers and garbage trucks are inevitable!) Verify the call-in number and test it. Dial-in a few minutes early for insurance. Know how to redial in a hurry in case you're disconnected. Have water handy. Arrange notes in front of you, including the participant names and your opening sentence. Now breathe. You're all set.

Star Power Tip #100

Have a tech-rehearsal prior to a live presentation, to diagnose and prevent mistakes from occurring during the actual performance. This can be quick, but it's vital. Talk directly with the *"AV"* (Audio-Visual) tech person who will be running equipment. (See Tip #26.) Rehearse your abbreviated presentation by the numbers, so he or she understands your needs and desired end results. Discuss specifics including audio and video requirements, music and light cues, microphone and sound system details, etc. If using PowerPoint, cue it up to the first slide and be clear on when to start it. Practice with the remote. Work the bugs out beforehand, so you can be worry free and ready to "wow" the audience.

Star Power Tip #101

Talent Release: Legal permission to use an individual's likeness. This is done by signature and date and becomes legally binding. *Have everyone sign a release before they leave*, including any audience member in the background whose face may appear on-camera. It's difficult to track people down after the fact. Don't jeopardize your time and production investment, and don't simply trust that minds won't change later. You'll be out of luck, even if you've spent a fortune editing the piece into a product or demo reel. Find a blank release document on the internet and have people sign it as they come in the door.

Star Power Tip #102

Get listed on the first page of Google! Video is the secret weapon. It's a game changer, boosting you higher and faster in search engine rankings. You may already have clips on your website and You Tube, but if no one is watching, they're not working. **Become Search Engine friendly.** Optimize videos using title, description, text captions, targeted and strategic key words, meta tags, links, location and annotations. Add *"Social Media"* to the mix too. It's the fastest, cheapest way to turbo-charge interaction and back links. Be consistent and creative to boost engagement, return visits, and viral sharing... and watch your popularity soar!

Star Power Tip #103

Don't let audio recording intimidate you. Many software packages for Macs and PCs allow you to **create your own professional sound studio**, ranging from easy to expert. Check the internet to see what's available, and look for "how to" video tutorials. *"Audacity"* is a free audio recorder and editor for Mac and Windows. *"Audio Acrobat"* lets you record through a telephone handset. *"FreeConferenceCall.com"* does too, and it's free. Or, get a microphone that plugs into the computer, and use a program like *"Sony Sound Forge."* Create audio products. Add audio messages to email and blogs. Record conference calls, teleclasses and interviews. Once you record the audio, it's easier than you think to add music for pizzazz and to enhance the product. (See Tip #70.)

Star Power Tip #104

When speaking directly after another speaker, if you're both using PowerPoint you'll probably need to share the same remote. Be prepared to make a quick grab! To make sure the remote doesn't get lost in the "going-coming" chaos (in case the other speaker exits on the other side of the stage, for instance), designate someone beforehand whose sole responsibility is to ***coordinate the remote handoff.*** It's one less thing to stress about.

Star Power Tip #105

When making a live presentation, remember... the buck stops with you. Think of yourself as a one-person show. Producer. Writer. Director. Star. (And glorified Go-fer.) Be self-contained. Don't leave anything to chance or assume something will be done. Make sure it is. It's important to **set your own props** so you know exactly where they are. Then do one final check before *"show time"* to verify all is correct. (Sometimes things accidentally get moved or removed.) You'll be front and center wearing egg on your face if something is missing or goes wrong.

Star Power Tip #106

Many times when hired to speak, you will be told the presentation will be taped. Don't count on it being done well enough to use as a *"Video Demo"* of your talk. Most often, the camera is placed in the back of the room and set on a wide shot, so you become a teeny, tiny ant in the big picture. Or, maybe the camera work is unprofessional, the lighting is off, and/or the audio is unusable. Disappointing when you're counting on quality video for repurposing! One more time: Image is everything. Hedge your bet – **hire a professional film crew** and do it the right way. (Not just your wife's brother-in-law, twice-removed.)

Star Power Tip #107

Intention, intention, intention! Oprah says that INTENTION is everything, so before you speak **get clear on exactly what you want to get out of this presentation or media opportunity**. Jack Barnard created this checklist: *What's the purpose of this appearance? What do you want your audience to receive? What do you want to get out of it for yourself? What must you do to make it happen? How much time do you have?* This list will help create the open, close, talking points and *"Call-to-Action."* Use it to quickly collect your thoughts, even for a spur-of-the moment speaking opportunity! In 30 seconds you can structure an impactful message that will yield the desired results for both you and your audience. With a strong intention and organized thinking, everything else will fall into place.

Star Power Tip #108

Become a pro in audio recording sessions. Drink lots of water, because the more you talk, the thicker saliva becomes. Keep apple slices handy, as pectin counteracts this effect. Avoid milk or dairy products before recording. Milk tends to produce mucous, which just plain sounds gross. If you start to lose your voice or get bothered by phlegm, sip hot water with lemon and honey. Don't keep trying to clear your throat, because it causes more irritation and goes downhill from there. Once your voice is stressed, you may have to stop and come back the next day. Another tip: Brush your teeth! You will enunciate better.

Star Power Tip #109

Holding a book or "prop" on-camera? Here's an insider trade secret. When bringing the item up into the shot, ***tip it forward and down at a 45-degree angle*** to the camera, to prevent lights from reflecting off the surface. This creates an optical illusion. The viewer won't register that it's tilted, and you'll ensure a clean shot with no light glare. Bring it up and down several times while watching the monitor to find the perfect arc and angle, and set your mark. (See Tip #32.) You must hit it the same way every time. Roll camera and shoot, then check playback afterward to make sure it's a *"clean take"* – with no shiny *"hot spots"* – before moving on to the next shot. (Check Tip #39 for more on displaying products on-camera.)

Star Power Tip #110

Hosting your own radio show can be a great way to promote business. However, all hosting platforms and sites are not created equal. When determining where to park your show, there are a few things to consider. Read the fine print and **make sure you own your content**. Most sites (even the most famous) require you to sign-off that they own content you create and host on their site, even if it's your intellectual property and you do all the interviews and work involved. This means **you may not be allowed to repurpose**, or if so, it must be used exactly "as is" utilizing their branding, logo and music intro. Negotiate and own your content above all else.

Star Power Tip #111

Best tip on the planet, saved for last! ***Feeling nervous, worried, frustrated and overwhelmed? Call me.*** I will train, coach and direct you on-camera, develop your message, and show you what to say and exactly how to say it. Work with me one-on-one, or attend a Workshop or Boot Camp. I'm available to consult, coach, mentor and support by phone or webcam. ***Need videos? Come to my L.A. studio*** and I'll walk you through the entire video development process from start to finish. You will take away newfound confidence and skills, as well as dynamic professional videos. You'll be astonished at your commanding, on-camera image and I guarantee, ***you will be thrilled with the results!***